SCHIRMER'S LIBRARY
OF MUSICAL CLASSICS

Vol. 1928

ERNEST SACHSE

One Hundred Studies

For Trumpet

**Edited by
Franz Herbst**

G. SCHIRMER, Inc.

DISTRIBUTED BY

CORPORATION

7777 W. BLUEMOUND RD. P.O. BOX 13819 MILWAUKEE, WI 53213

One Hundred Studies

For Trumpet

Edited by
Franz Herbst

ERNEST SACHSE

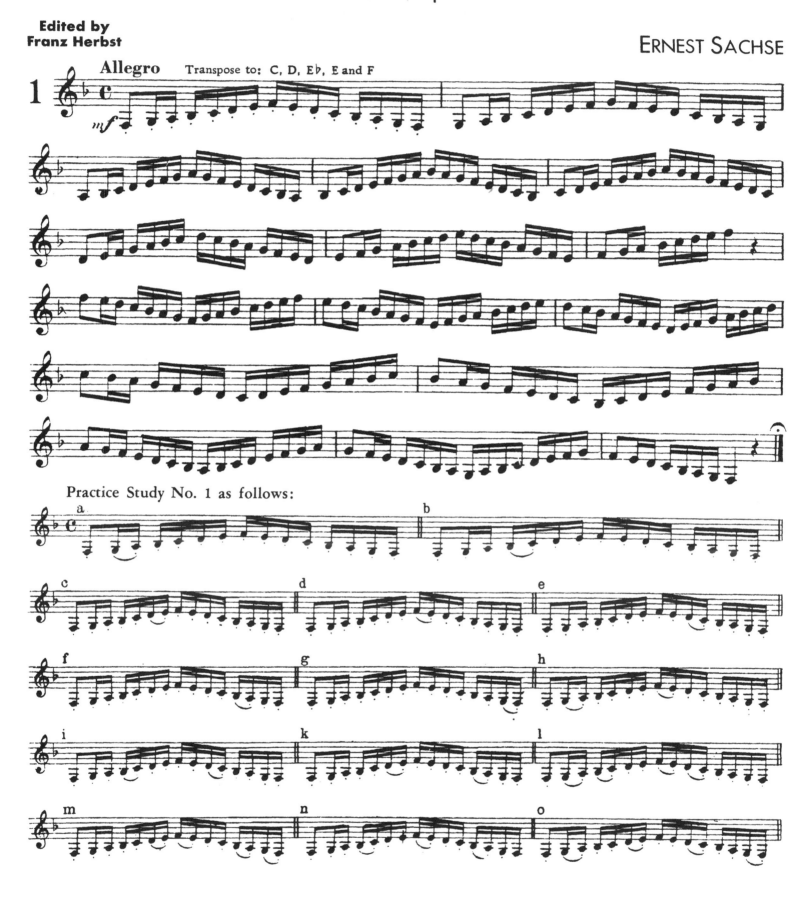

Practice Study No. 1 as follows:

4

Allegro Transpose to: A♭, A, C, D, E♭, E and F

4

Practice Study No. 4 as follows:

a   b   c

Allegro. Transpose to: A♭, A, C, D, E♭, E and F

5

Practice Study No. 5 as follows:

Allegretto   Transpose to : A, C, D, E♭, E and F

6

Practice Study No. 6 as follows:

Practice Study No. 8 as follows:

Transpose to: A, C, D, E♭, E and F

Moderato

9

8

Moderato Transpose to: A, C, D, E♭, E and F

10

Allegro vivace Transpose to: A, C, D, E♭, E and F

11

Allegro vivace Transpose to: Ab, A, C, D, Eb, E and F

13

Moderato Transpose to: Eb and F

14

Adagio con espressione Transpose to: A♭, A, C, D, E♭, E and F

19

Allegro Transpose to: C, D and E♭

20

* |-indicates breath marks

Vivace Transpose to: C, D, E♭ and F

21

Allegretto = ♪ = Transpose to: A♭, A, C, D, E♭ and F

24

18

Moderato Transpose to: A, C, D, E♭ and F

26

Andante Transpose to: A♭, A, C, D, E, E♭ and F

27

Larghetto = ♪ = Transpose to: A♭, A, C, D, E, E♭ and F
Con espressione.

30

Allegro Transpose to: Ab, A, C, D, E, Eb and F

31

Presto

Transpose to: C, D, Eb and F

32

Allegro Transpose to: A♭, A, C, D, E♭, E and F

33

Allegro vivace Transpose to: A, C, D, Eb and F

34

Transpose to: A, C, D, E, Eb and F
Con espressione.

Andante

37

Andante

Transpose to: E♭ and F

42

43 **Moderato** Transpose to : A, C, D and Eb

Allegro non tanto Transpose to: C, D, Eb and F

47

Allegro animato Transpose to: E♭ and F

48

Moderato Transpose to: C, D, E♭ and F

49

Allegro Transpose to: D and E♭

51

Transpose to: Ab, A, C, Db and D

Moderato

52

p

Con Moto Transpose to: C, D♭ and D

53

Allegro moderato Transpose to: C, D, Eb, E and F

54

Transpose to: Ab, A, C, Db, D and Eb

57 Moderato

Allegro Transpose to: E♭ and D♭

58

Moderato

Transpose to: A and C

59

Allegro Transpose to: E♭ and F

60

Moderato Transpose to: A and C

62

Allegretto Transpose to: C and D

63

Allegretto Transpose to: E♭

64

Allegro Transpose to: Eb

65

Presto Transpose to: E♭

66

Allegro Transpose to: Ab, A and Eb

69

Presto Transpose to: C and D

72

Moderato Transpose to: C and D

73

Allegro moderato Transpose to: E♭

77

ad lib.

64

espressivo

86 **Moderato** Transpose to: A, C and D

Allegro non troppo Transpose to: D and F

87

88 **Allegro** Transpose to: D and F

89 **Prestissimo** Transpose to: D and F

Allegro moderato

Transpose to: D and F

90

cre - - scen - - do   f

p

Allegro agitato Transpose to: D and F

91

Transpose to: A♭ and A

94 **Allegro**

Allegro Transpose to: E♭ and A

95

Andante con moto Transpose to: E♭, A♭ and A

96

Allegretto grazioso Transpose to: E♭

97

Transpose to: A, C, D and G (low)

100